Tell Me, Papa

Answers to questions children ask about death and dying

A Centering Corporation Resource by Joy and Dr. Marvin Johnson

Illustrated by Anne Catharine Blake

www.centering.org

Centering Corporation
PO Box 4600
Omaha, NE 68104

Phone: 402-553-1200
Fax: 402-553-0507

Printed in Canada

This book is dedicated to our Papas,
Roy and Stuart,
who gave us the gift of answers to our questions.

Our thanks to the people who helped Papa

Dr. Robert Slater, our freinds at the Hastings Regional Center,
Jerrie Jones, Rabbi Paul Drazen, Susie Drazen, Sharon Turnbull,
Diane, Amber and Matt Ferrara,
our own children and Percy Grey-Paws, who was a real cat and much loved.

Hello there! I'm a grandpa.
My children call me PAPA.
You can call me PAPA, too.

I want to tell you about something.
I want to tell you about death.
I want to tell you what happens.
I want to tell you about funerals and saying goodbye.

4

Tell me, Papa.

First of all, it is good to know about death. Death is a part of life.
Everyone and everything dies at some time.

When someone we love dies, we have a lot of feelings,
like the time my grandchildren found our dead cat.
It was our old cat, Percy Grey-Paws. He was dead under a tree.

The children had a lot of feelings.
Jim was afraid. He wanted to pretend it didn't happen.
Janet was angry. She thought someone had killed Percy.
Jenny thought maybe she had done something to make Percy die.

In the night, Jenny came into her Mom and Dad's room.
She cried some more.
She wanted to dig Percy up and tell him to be alive again.

When a person we love - - or a good pet - - dies, we have a lot of feelings.
We have big feelings.
We have sad feelings, mad feelings;
sometimes we think we have bad feelings.

All our feelings are OK. All our feelings are real.
All our feelings, the big ones and the little ones, are important.

It's important to know what happens when someone has died.

Tell me, Papa.

When someone dies, everything inside of that person stops.
The heart stops.
The breathing stops.
The thinking and feeling stops.

When a person is dead, that person cannot think about things.
They cannot feel any hurt. They cannot feel hot or cold.

When we are dead, we do not have any life in our bodies anymore.
What is left is just the body.

Like a peanut shell without the peanut.

Like an apple peel with no apple.

Like a school with no children.

But the body that is left is important. The body is dead, and needs to be taken care of.

To do that, we call a person who knows how to take care of the bodies of dead people.

That person is a Funeral Director.

Some funeral directors are dads. Some funeral directors are moms.
The funeral director has gone to a special school to learn how to take care of bodies.

He goes to where the person died and carefully lifts the body onto a stretcher.
He covers the body and bundles it snugly onto the stretcher.

Then the funeral director wheels the stretcher, body and all,
into a big car and drives to the funeral home.

A funeral home is a very big and very nice house.
It is fixed up to take care of the bodies of people we love.

As soon as the funeral director gets to the funeral home,
she takes the body into a very clean, special room.

It is called the preparation room.
This is where she will get the body ready for the funeral.

The funeral director keeps the body safe.
Sometimes special people come to help the funeral director.
They may help wash the body.
They will work carefully to get the body ready for the funeral.

When the body is all ready, it is gently placed in the casket.
The casket is a box that is different from all other boxes.
It is built to hold the body.
It looks very nice.
Some families have a casket where the top is open so you can see the body.
Other families close the casket and it is not opened again.

The body inside the casket will look good.
The body will look asleep.

Remember though, being dead and being asleep are not alike.
When we are asleep, our parts inside keep working, making us ready
for the next day.

We move. We breathe in and out. We toss and turn.

The dead body does not move.
The parts inside have stopped, and the body is ready for the funeral.

If your family has the casket open you can look at the body.
You can tell the difference between being dead and being asleep.

If your family has an open casket, you can touch the body if you want.
It will feel cool and the skin will feel firm.
It will feel a lot like the cover of this book, smooth and cool.
It's all right to look at the body or the casket as much as you want to.

This is part of saying goodbye to the dead person.
Another way to say goodbye to the dead person we love is at a funeral or memorial service.

A funeral is a way to say goodbye and thank you.
What happens next depends on your family's way of saying goodbye.

Whatever way you have of saying goodbye, people will come to see you.
Some will come to your house.
Some may come before the funeral; others may come afterwards.
Some will just come for the funeral.

People may bring food. They may bring flowers.
There may even be relatives you have never met,
or some you have forgotten.
There will be lots of family and friends you know.
They may cry together and hug each other.
Some will probably hug you and say how you have grown.

The story of your loved one's life and death will be told many times.
Telling it helps the sad get better.

Sometimes it may seem like no one is paying attention to you at all.

That is OK, too.

Big people have a lot to think about after someone dies.
There is a lot of planning. There are many decisions.
Soon someone will be ready to talk with you and listen to you.

When it is time for the funeral, everyone will go where the service is held.

The service may be at the funeral home.
It may be at the place where you worship.
Sometimes the service is all at the cemetery.

The casket will be there with the body in it.
There may be flowers around the casket.
People will sit together.
The family may sit in a place just for the family.

There may be music.
There will be a short talk about the dead person.
A minister, priest or rabbi may say prayers and talk about what death means.

And people may cry. Crying is OK.
Crying helps the sad get better, too.
Whenever you feel like crying after someone has died, it is OK.

You may get restless at the funeral. Sometimes funerals seem long for children.
It will be over soon. You will feel better because you went to the funeral.
You will feel better because you said goodbye.

When the funeral is over, everyone will go outside. Family and friends will get into the cars.
Soon the casket will be carried out.

It will be loaded carefully into a big, big car. The big car is called a hearse.
Its job is to carry the body.

It will move slowly away from where the funeral service was held.
All the cars will follow the hearse.
It will go to a cemetery.

Now it is time to bury the body.

When you get to the cemetery you will see chairs, a tent top, and a big, neat hole in the ground. The hole in the ground is called a grave.

You will feel the breeze in the cemetery and smell the good outdoor smells.

There will be more words and prayers. When all the words have been said, the funeral is over.

Now people can say their last goodbye to the dead person.

Most people say goodbye without using words. It is all right to say goodbye out loud, too.

Sometimes the casket is lowered carefully into the grave while
family and friends are still there.
At other times everyone leaves first, and then special people
place the casket in the grave.

Some people say goodbye by putting some of the tender earth into the grave.
Others will take a flower from on or near the casket.
Finally, the casket will be covered with the good, rich earth dug just for it.

It will stay there, and be safe.

You may want to come back and see the grave again, at some time.

Maybe your person's body was not buried.
There are other things families do to take care of the body.
Sometimes families have the body cremated.

When a body is cremated, the funeral director carefully wraps the body
and takes it to a special place called a crematorium.
A person caring for the body carefully puts the body into a special box.
The box goes into a very small room.

When the body is safe inside the room, the caring person goes out, carefully closing the door.
When the caring person is outside the room, she pushes a little button.

The little button starts a very hot fire inside the little room. The fire changes the body.
The body begins to gently melt into soft ashes.
It is something like an ice cream cone that melts from the inside out. All that is left is ashes.

The person caring for the body gently picks up the ashes.
The ashes are put into a special machine. The machine makes them smaller.
Now the ashes look like ground-up seashells or very large bits sand.

The ashes are finally put into a beautiful jar. The jar is called an urn.
If your special person's body is cremated, your family will have a special place for the urn.
Maybe you can see the urn and ask more questions.

Your family can do many very nice things with the ashes.
Some people scatter the ashes over a favorite place.
Some people bury the urn or keep it in a special little house at the cemetery.
Some people keep a tiny bit of the ashes in a special piece of jewelry or in a tiny box.

All these ways of taking care of your loved one's body are good.
All these ways of saying goodbye are good, too.

You will have said goodbye to someone who meant something to you.
You will have felt the big feelings that come when someone dies.
You will have been a part of your family in a very special way.

When you have questions, ask someone in your family.
If you have questions about the body, ask your family, or ask your funeral director.
He wants to help you.

If you have questions about what happens to the alive part of a person when a person dies,
ask your family. your minister or your rabbi.

Some people believe that dying is like walking through a door into a place we can't see when we are alive.

These beliefs are important. It is important for you to know them.

Beliefs help us when someone dies. Dying may be a new beginning. It is good for you to know about endings and beginnings. It is good to know about living and dying.

PERCY GREY-PAWS

I want to thank you. Thank you for letting me tell you about death.
Thank you for letting me tell you about funerals and about saying goodbye.

You are a fine person.
You are a good listener.
I have enjoyed talking with you.

Thank You, Papa!

About the Authors

In 1978, Joy and Dr. Marvin Johnson founded Centering Corporation. Since then, Centering has become a well-respected, worldwide grief resource center. The Johnsons live in Omaha, Nebraska, and have 6 children and 7 grandchildren.

About the Illustrator

Anne Catharine Blake has illustrated over a dozen books for children, including *Josh's Smiley Faces: A Story about Anger and the Child's Guide* series. She studied book illustration and design in Canada, France and, most recently, Syracuse University's in New York. She lives in Oregon with her two cats, George and Gracie.

For Ma, Sylvia Hoffman who answered my questions
with honesty, optimism, and much humor.

www.centering.org